The great question is then: Why, if we have a project that favors the immense majority, does this not translate into an equivalent social and electoral support? The explanation we often give is that conservative forces use the media to disseminate a deformed vision of our project. But we are also at fault for this misunderstanding. We have not been able to explain to the people the real dimensions of our project in terms they can understand. And worst of all, our lives have not been coherent with our project. We preach democracy but we act in an authoritarian way; we want to build a solidarian society but we are selfish; we advocate for the defense of nature but we are consumerists. If we want to convince, we need to change ourselves as well.

> Marta Harnecker and Tassos Tsakiroglou:
> "A New Revolutionary Subject,"
> *Monthly Review* 71,
> no. 5 (October 2019):58–62
> (https://monthlyreview. org/2019/
> 10/01/a-new-revolutionary-subject-2/).

Rinky-Dink Revolution

RINKY-DINK REVOLUTION

Moving Beyond Capitalism by Withholding Consent, Creative Constructions, and Creative Destructions

Howard Waitzkin

Published by Daraja Press
https://darajapress.com
in association with
MR Essays
https://mronline.org/category/monthly-review-essays/
© 2020 Howard Waitzkin
ISBN (soft cover) : 978-1-988832-53-1
ISBN (ebook): 978-1-988832-54-8

Library and Archives of Canada Catalog in Publishing data

Title: Rinky-dink revolution : moving beyond capitalism by withholding consent, creative constructions, and creative destructions / Howard Waitzkin.
Names: Waitzkin, Howard, author.
Description: Includes bibliographical references.
Identifiers: Canadiana (print) 20190241349 | Canadiana (ebook) 20200070010 | ISBN 9781988832531 (softcover) | ISBN 9781988832548 (ebook)
Subjects: LCSH: Anti-globalization movement.
Classification: LCC HM881 .W35 2020 | DDC 303.48/4—dc23

Book design by Kate McDonnell
Diagrams designed by Mira Lee

Contents

Moving beyond capitalism now **8**

Peculiar ways to struggle without confronting capitalism **12**

Rinky-dink revolution and revolutionaries **21**

Creative constructions **36**

Creative destructions **49**

The death of capitalism and the birth of something else **65**

About the author **68**

Acknowledgments **69**

Vision statement: Moving beyond capitalism—now!
Howard Waitzkin and Firoze Manji **70**

Moving beyond
capitalism now

During this fierce period of history, many people want clarity and leadership in suggesting concrete steps toward ending the daily oppressions of capitalism. We seek a path leading to a post-capitalist society that aims not to destroy mother earth, humanity, and other life forms. If that doesn't happen, we face an ongoing transition to fascism and an accelerating environmental catastrophe. These stakes have become much easier to understand for inhabitants of planet earth, and dire predictions about our fate have become commonplace. One of the most eloquent is István Mészáros's statement about the "Leviathan" that comprises the capitalist state: "… a way must be found to extricate humanity from the ever more dangerous—in fact potentially in a literal sense self-annihilating—arbitrary decision-making practices of the Leviathan state. There can be no hope for the survival of humanity without that."[1]

And yet, the path of how to move from capitalism to post-capitalism continues to baffle even the most brilliant and devoted revolutionaries. "It's easier to imagine the end of the world than the end of our economic system." This statement, attributed to Fredric Jameson, conveys how simple it is to visualize scenarios leading to the end of humanity and other beings (global warming with rising oceans and hot, uninhabitable land masses; nuclear armageddon with radioactivity killing almost all animals and plants; etc.)[2] The quote also conveys a vacuum of creative thinking that continues

---

[1] István Mészáros, "Preface to *Beyond Leviathan*," *Monthly Review* 69, no. 9 (February 2019): 47-57.
[2] Fredric Jameson, "Future City," *New Left Review* 21 (May-June 2003): 65-79.

to stand in the way of moving beyond global capitalism, which each year benefits an ever tinier part of the world's population (now roughly 0.5 percent).

Answering the question of how to get from A to B, capitalism to post-capitalism, is a task that we "audaciously" need to pursue now.³ Mészáros and those influenced by his work on transition "beyond capital," in Venezuela and elsewhere, have grappled with this question and have achieved as of yet incomplete results, given the dynamics associated with global capitalism and imperialism.⁴ We no longer can comfort ourselves with the claim that future generations will solve the problem, even if we ourselves don't live long enough to enjoy the solution. We must take on this historical challenge once again, even though revolutionaries spanning Marxism, anarchism, utopianism, and other traditions, with only a few exceptions, have tried and failed thus far to overcome capitalism as an economic system and the leviathan state as the enforcer of that system.

We are living in revolutionary times. The present contains tremendous dangers: nuclear war, global warming and other environmental catastrophes, and fascism—a world based on deepening expropriation of

---

3 For an inspiring discussion of audacity and the need for more of it, see Samir Amin, *The Implosion of Contemporary Capitalism* (New York: Monthly Review Press, 2013).
4 István Mészáros, *Beyond Capital* (New York: Monthly Review Press, 2010), especially chapters 13, 19, and 20. For helpful discussions of applications of Mészáros's work in Venezuela's Bolivarian Revolution, especially about communal transition, see: John Bellamy Foster, "Chávez and the Communal State: On the Transition to Socialism in Venezuela," *Monthly Review* 66, no. 11 (April 2015): 1–17; Michael Lebowitz, *The Socialist Imperative* (New York: Monthly Review Press, 2015), chapters 5–6; and Marta Harnecker, *A World To Build* (New York: Monthly Review Press, 2015), chapters 7–9.

nature, inequality, repression, and suffering. These dangers have also generated global resistance and social movements aiming to create a world based on harmony with nature, cooperative relationships of mutual aid, and decision-making by ordinary people about the directions our societies will take.

Who am I to write about how revolution might happen? Whatever I have achieved doesn't qualify me over anybody else in trying figure out how to get from A to B. I intend this pamphlet as one among others, as we struggle to move from capitalism to post-capitalism. For hopes about others' efforts, please see the vision statement at the end of this pamphlet.

Peculiar ways to struggle without **confronting capitalism**

Because it is hard to imagine a viable path from capitalism to post-capitalism, most people who try to address our world's challenges assume that capitalism will continue to exist. So, those of us oppressed by capitalism engage in some peculiar forms of actions and inactions. In our actions, we take part in struggles to improve key problems generated by capitalism without confronting capitalism, even though we recognize that capitalism generates the problems and continues to make them worse (Figure 1).

In other words, our actions confront effects rather than causes. Here are only some of the social problems that capitalism causes, directly or indirectly:

1. Tremendously unequal distribution of income and wealth, leading to poverty, inequality, food insecurity, and housing insecurity;
2. Conflicts among peoples fomented and manipulated by elites, including racism, sexism, ageism, and other isms based on socially constructed differences;
3. Militarism, endless war, gun violence, the arms trade, and the military-industrial complex, which have become a key arena for the accumulation of capital through cycles of destruction and reconstruction (designated by Naomi Klein and others as "disaster capitalism"[1]);
4. Environmental degradation, pollution, the climate crisis, and species extinction, which result from capitalism's inherent need to expropriate natural resources causing a metabolic rift in the earth's ecological balance;

---

[1] Naomi Klein, *The Shock Doctrine* (New York: Metropolitan, 2007), especially parts 3, 5–7.

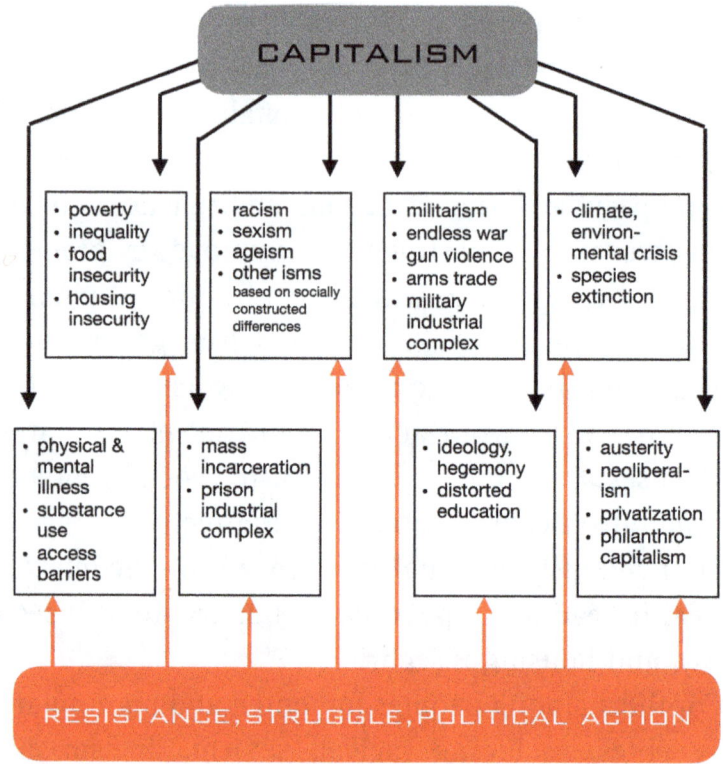

Figure 1. Peculiar Ways of Struggling to Improve Our Key Problems Without Confronting Capitalism

5 Distorted education, designed to reinforce hegemonic ideologies that favor the interests of elites;

6 Ill health, mental illness and emotional suffering, drug use, barriers to accessible services, the medical-industrial complex, and social determinants of illness and early death that derive from the inequalities and insecurities of our political-economic system;

7 Mass incarceration and the prison-industrial complex; and

8 Policies of neoliberalism, austerity, privatization, and philanthrocapitalism, which weaken public-sector institutions and services for vulnerable populations

while benefiting those who own and control private, for-profit corporations.

Faced with the suffering that capitalism causes in these and other arenas, activists worldwide engage in resistance, struggle, and political action within each arena but usually ignore or de-emphasize the root causes of each problem in capitalism. Environmentalists try to protect the environment against particular toxic onslaughts of capital, such as fossil fuels, plastics, fracking, pesticides, and so forth, without confronting the inherent expropriation of nature by the global capitalist system.[2] Struggles against racism and sexism address these oppressions as problems in themselves, rather than tracing and fighting their root causes in capitalism, for instance in recognizing that capitalism from the beginning has flourished through slavery, genocide, subjugation of women, and promotion of socially constructed ideologies about race and gender that keep oppressed peoples from uniting.[3] Regarding health, we in the U.S.A. struggle for single-payer systems like improved Medicare for all, without coming

---

2 Fred Magdoff and John Bellamy Foster, *What Every Environmentalist Needs to Know about Capitalism* (New York: Monthly Review Press, 2011); John Bellamy Foster and Brett Clark, "The Robbery of Nature: Introduction," *Monthly Review* 70, no. 3 (July-August 2018) and other essays in this issue, https://monthlyreview.org/2018/07/01/mr-070-03-2018-07_0/#lightbox/0/.

3 For a very partial selection of helpful sources: Gerald Horne, *The Apocalypse of Settler Colonialism: The Roots of Slavery, White Supremacy, and Capitalism in Seventeenth-Century North America and the Caribbean* (New York: Monthly Review Press, 2018); Roxane Dunbar-Ortiz, *An Indigenous Peoples' History of the United States* (Boston: Beacon Press, 2015); Silvia Federici, *Revolution at Point Zero* (Oakland, CA: PM Press, 2012); Tithi Bhattacharya, ed., *Social Reproduction Theory* (London: Pluto, 2017). These sources and others clarify that slavery, racialization, genocide, and gender oppression existed before capitalism but became key components of capitalism's success story.

to grips with the continuing vulnerability of national health programs within capitalist states, as we have seen recently throughout Europe.[4] Similar uncomfortable observations apply to all the other arenas of struggle on the list.

Occasionally as activists we tip our hats to the importance of overcoming capitalism, for instance in claiming that we want to create "non-reformist reforms." From this viewpoint, such reforms are not end points in themselves but rather generate continuing contradictions and frustrations that lead to further revolutionary struggle. Most often, though, the linkages between reform and revolution remain vague, as they have throughout history.[5] The cognitive problem persists that we don't clarify precisely how our organizing around targeted reforms actually will lead to revolution, that is, how we move from capitalism to post-capitalism, from A to B. The fragility of reforms accomplished within capitalist states, as seen for instance in the dismantling of European national health programs and the reversal of many other successful reforms under austerity policies, also leads to questions about the wisdom of such reform struggles as the main focus, as opposed to struggles that more directly attack the smooth functioning of capitalism and that stand a chance of transforming it.

---

4 Adam Gaffney and Carles Muntaner, "Austerity and Health Care," in Howard Waitzkin and the Working Group on Health Beyond Capitalism, *Health Care Under the Knife: Moving Beyond Capitalism for Our Health* (New York: Monthly Review Press, 2018).

5 André Gorz, *Socialism and Revolution* (New York: Anchor, 1973), pp. 135-177; Rosa Luxemburg, *Reform or Revolution* (London: Militant Publications, 1908), https://www.marxists.org/archive/luxembur5rtif@it00/reform-revolution/index.htm

In addition to our contradictory actions, our inactions involve consent. We consent by not challenging or even trying to change our simple economic behaviors that perpetuate the capitalist economic system. As a result, we ordinary people continue to serve as the main financiers of the capitalist system, in several ways. First, we continue to rely on the "FIRE" industry—finance, insurance, and real estate—for our savings and retirement funds, home and car loans, educational loans, credit and debit cards, checking accounts, insurance policies, internet purchases, and most other everyday financial transactions and long-term investments. While we despise these parasitic corporations for their greedy behaviors, and while we understand that they transfer our own money into the corporations that preside over each problematic arena of the capitalist system listed in Figure 1, we rarely take the initiative to withhold our funds from their use.

Similarly, we obediently pay our taxes, even though we understand that they go mainly to help the capitalist state prop up the capitalist economic system. In particular, about half of our income taxes pay for present and past wars.[6] Despite a progressive tax framework in which the rich pay proportionately more, loopholes make the actual U.S. income tax system regressive, so that in fact the poor pay proportionately more. Many wealthy individuals and corporations pay little or no taxes. Facing such unfair and harmful taxation requirements, thousands of people resist some or all of their

---

6 War Resisters League, "Where Your Income Tax Money Really Goes," https://www.warresisters.org.

income taxes, including many like myself who conscientiously object to paying for war. Tax resistance has figured as an important part of U.S. history, including resistance to the taxes imposed on colonists by the British government through the Stamp Act, Tea Act, and other taxes in the lead up to the first U.S. Revolution. Despite widespread anger and frustration with taxes in the United States, most taxpayers consent.

Why do oppressed people consent to their oppression? Consent to capitalism and the reasons for it have fascinated anti-capitalists. Although brutal repression can and does achieve consent in some situations, usually it is not enough, as Gramsci observed while imprisoned by Italian fascism. In addition to violence, dictatorships survive and flourish because people believe in the principles that they stand for. Most explanations of consent have focused on some variation of ideology, the "hegemonic" ideas that oppressed people learn and that explain and justify the oppressive circumstances of our lives.[7] Those in the class that dominates promote these ideas in many ways, including religious beliefs that interpret why some people suffer and others don't, schooling that teaches principles of merit and hierarchy, professionals—in medicine, psychiatry, law, criminal justice, the military—who act on behalf of the dominant class to persuade or coerce us to follow norms of acceptable behavior, and media like television and the internet. Ideology conveys powerful messages that lack of consent is unethical, impious, sick, deviant, unfash-

---

[7] Antonio Gramsci, *Selections from the Prison Notebooks* (New York: International, 1971), Part 3.

ionable, illegal, and dangerous, and that common sense involves accepting "there is no alternative" (TINA for short) to capitalism.

Ideology also involves beliefs about democracy. Specifically, ideology educates the public that a government controlled by the capitalist class is democratic and that elections giving power to that class are fair. Voters' longing for humane government and responsive leadership chosen through elections has rarely been realized, if ever. Since the claimed origins of democracy during the Athenian empire, with rare exceptions, elections have remained the tool of rich and powerful elites. The critique of "bourgeois democracy" runs from Marx (who pointed out that indigenous societies like the Iroquois Confederacy developed much more meaningful democratic participation in political decision making), to V.I. Lenin (who quoted Marx in saying, "Every once in a while, the oppressed are allowed to decide which particular representatives of the oppressing class will represent them, and oppress them"), to Tommy Douglas (Canada's left-wing politician, who initiated its national health program and spoke in Parliament about "Mouseland," where mice vote for black cats or white cats but never for mice), and more, but an aphorism attributed to Emma Goldman sums up the argument: "if voting changed anything, they'd have made it illegal long ago." Yet ideology teaches us that we can improve the harmful effects of capitalism by voting for good candidates who promise to do that.

As poverty, inequality, food insecurity, job insecurity, racism, sexism, militarism, the threat of nuclear war, the climate crisis and environmental catastrophe, ideology, unmet needs for medical and mental health services, mass incarceration, and neoliberal austerity policies persist and worsen, millions of people throughout the world now realize that limited reforms in capitalism will not work. They/we are ready to move ahead on the path beyond capitalism. The path involves radical transformations leading to a post-capitalist economic system.

How can that happen? Answering this question and then acting on the answers have emerged as the central challenges of praxis—the quest to unify theory and practice—for thinkers and activists concerned about planet earth and the beings who live here. It is time to shift our approach to confronting capitalism directly as the cause of the intractable problems that we face, rather than only trying to improve capitalism's noxious effects. In doing so, we begin to imagine how to move beyond capitalism and then to move along that path.

Rinky-dink revolution
and revolutionaries

Rinky-dink revolution involves actions and inactions that are easy and predictably safe, at least for the most part. (*Rinky-dink*, a term used more commonly in the United States than in other countries, refers to simple actions that are so easy and safe to do that anyone can do them. These are the day-to-day revolutionary actions needed during this critical period of history.) Such actions are mundane, unglamorous, and feasible within every person's life. They are much less romantic than the heroic examples of some prior revolutions, when the capitalist class violently repressed relatively small groups of revolutionaries, who then organized and fought back with violence that eventually became victorious. Rather than heroism, rinky-dink revolution demands ordinary actions and inactions by ordinary people who do not seek to be remembered in books or on tee-shirts.

Imagining the end of our economic system and then the actual creation of a new one have to be simple, low risk, and doable by about 7 to 11 million people in the United States, the third most populous country in the world after China and India. Why 7 to 11 million, among a total U.S. population of more than 328 million people?[1] And how many committed revolutionaries would it take for revolution to happen in other, less populous capitalist countries?

The history of revolutions shows that the activists who bring them about number much fewer than countries' entire populations. The proportion of a population

---

[1] U.S. Census Bureau Current Population, March 31, 2019, https://www.census.gov/popclock/print.php?component=counter.

needed to bring about a revolution of course depends on historical circumstances. It also depends on the "topdown" versus "bottom-up" dialectic of leadership and power. In the Soviet Union, China, Vietnam, and multiple countries of Latin America and Africa, revolutions have vacillated between tendencies to implement top-down, elite governance by self-appointed leaders considering themselves a vanguard, versus tendencies to implement decentralized, participatory, equalitarian, and more radically democratic governance. When they have failed, revolutions aiming to replace capitalism usually have collapsed due to a combination of external destabilization or direct military invasion by capitalist regimes, and/or inability to resolve the dialectic of top-down versus bottom-up governance.[2]

Considering the importance of the question about how many revolutionaries would it take, the answer should have become fairly clear by now, but actually very few meaningful estimates have appeared, with some exceptions. And the difficulty of resolving Jameson's paradox ("it's easier to imagine the end of the world than the end of our economic system") comes partly from our fears that we never could convince a large enough part of the population to support moving beyond capitalism. One exception comes from research on nonviolent resistance to dictatorships. Surprisingly, that work concluded that only about 3.5 percent of a

---

[2] For more on top-down versus bottom-up leadership: Marta Harnecker and José Bartolomé, *Planning from Below: A Decentralized Participatory Planning Proposal* (New York: Monthly Review Press, 2019); Howard Waitzkin, "Revolution Now: Teachings from the Global South for Revolutionaries in the Global North," *Monthly Review* 69, no. 6 (November 2018): 18-36.

population can topple a brutal dictatorship in a capitalist regime.³ In their organizing, Cooperation Jackson in Mississippi is aiming for a 20 percent participation rate (which includes people who are actively participating but are not leaders). These folks are struggling to bring about revolutionary transformation in a city and the region; leaders encourage other community members to participate in popular assemblies and other processes of radical democracy. Cooperation Jackson's experience so far indicates that substantial movement beyond capitalism can happen with a regular participation rate actually lower than that.⁴

The estimate of 7 to 11 million people required to achieve revolutionary transformation in the United States comes from a simple calculation, which may be off, but probably not way off. If the relevant population of the United States includes eligible voters (231,557,000 as of the 2016 election), using 5 percent as a more conservative figure than the 3.5 percent found in research, that would involve about 11,578,000 nonviolently resisting individuals. If instead the relevant population includes registered voters who actually voted in the 2016 presidential election (138,885,000), fundamental change could happen through concerted

---

3 Erica Chenoweth and Maria J. Stephan, *Why Civil Resistance Works* (New York: Columbia University Press, 2012); Erica Chenoweth, "It May Only Take 3.5% of the Population to Topple a Dictator—with Civil Resistance," *Guardian*, February 1, 2017, https://www.theguardian.com/commentisfree/2017/feb/01/worriedamerican-democracy-study-activist-techniques.

4 Kali Akuno, "Cooperation Jackson," presented at The Left Forum, New York, June 2018. For further details, see Kali Akuno and Ajamu Nangwaya, *Jackson Rising: The Struggle for Economic Democracy and Black Self-Determination in Jackson, Mississippi* (Montreal, Canada: Daraja Press, 2017) and later here in the section on "creative constructions."

nonviolent action by about seven million people. Similar calculations would lead to a conclusion that in capitalist countries with much smaller populations, proportionally fewer revolutionaries could achieve this kind of dramatic change. Even if the calculation underestimates the revolutionary forces by a factor of two or three times, such as Cooperation Jackson's 20 percent figure, the participants still would total a small minority of the population. And what about the repression that we could expect from a capitalist class in such trouble? It is not likely that the capitalist state could organize enough repression to imprison or kill 7 to 11 million revolutionaries, totaling more than those killed in the holocaust of World War II, especially for revolutionary activities as rinky-dink as those to be proposed here.

Who are the protagonists of rinky-dink revolution? That is, who are we, the revolutionaries, who make up that as yet unknown part of the population who will succeed in moving beyond capitalism? Who are they, against whom we revolt? A disappointing revelation for many of us who have tried to advance revolutionary change is that the old categories to which we are attached (electoral democracy, working class, left party, revolutionary vanguard, violent takeover of the state, etc.) are unlikely to help much during our current period of history, and maybe never have worked well. These categories, which have served as compelling guides for radical politics partly because of the persuasive rhetoric and heroic struggles advanced by some leaders using these terms, no longer illumine the transition to post-capitalism.

"They" are easier to understand than "we." "They" represent the less than 1 percent of the world's population who benefit from global capitalism, do not acknowledge its adverse effects, and resist change. A larger proportion of the world's population sell their labor to protect the capitalist class through repression and threats of repression. These people include military and paramilitary forces, police forces, the military-industrial complex, and the criminal justice system. Their weapons, especially nuclear weapons, help achieve consent through violence and fear of violence. But because repression is not enough to achieve consent, the capitalist class hires even more people to safeguard the system through ideological work. By their paid labor in the educational system, the media, the medical and mental health industries, and other components of the welfare state, these workers teach people "hegemonic" ideas: that there is no alternative to capitalism, that some people are enemies (racial minorities, immigrants, and additional subgroups who become the threatening other), and that if a person isn't happy and successful it is his or her own fault.[5] But even with their repressive protectors and shapers of false consciousness, "they" still make up a tiny proportion of the world's peoples.

Understanding who "we" are has become more challenging, as the old categories have become less convincing and helpful. "We" as revolutionary subjects have become much more expansive than previously.

---

[5] Influential analyses of such ideological work include: Gramsci, *Selections from the Prison Notebooks*; Louis Althusser, *Lenin and Philosophy and Other Essays* (New York: Monthly Review Press, 1971); Richard Sennett and Jonathan Cobb, *The Hidden Injuries of Class* (New York: Knopf, 1972).

The working class—those among us who do not control the means of production and must sell our labor to capitalists in order to survive—has become very diverse and, especially when represented by large labor unions, often more interested in incremental improvements of capitalism rather than moving beyond capitalism as an economic system.[6] Instead, the most active revolutionaries worldwide currently include people who don't fit well at all into the traditional categories. Today's revolutionary forces encompass members of the "precariate," mostly young people who hold precarious jobs that usually are impermanent, part-time, and without benefits such as health care and retirement pensions and who see no future for themselves in capitalism, even if highly educated. Other key revolutionary groups involve indigenous peoples whose lands and natural resources continue to be expropriated by global capitalism; racial and ethnic minority groups who have endured slavery and genocide during the growth of capitalism and who continue to experience oppressions of many kinds; and people in the so-called informal sector who survive hand to mouth even without regular wages earned by selling their labor to capitalists.

Some of the most influential revolutions worldwide involve radical communities whose members are not selling their daily work to capitalists and who receive inspiration from indigenous roots and anarchist ideas that spurn the capitalist or post-capitalist state, as in

---

6 Michael D. Yates clarifies the contradictions and potentialities of the current global working class in *Can the Working Class Change the World?* (New York: Monthly Review Press, 2018).

the Zapatista and Rojava revolutions.[7] Although the traditional working class may become part of the new "revolutionary subject," people who want and need revolution now go beyond the key protagonists as envisioned by Marx and Engels. And regarding revolutionary left parties, partly due to repression, they consistently have been diverted into trying to reform capitalism especially by participating in electoral politics, and revolutionary vanguards usually have failed also due to repression in addition to their inability to resolve the dialectic of top-down versus bottom-up revolutionary struggle.

In addition to financing capitalism, as noted earlier, we also are the millions who want a post-capitalist society that does not destroy mother earth, humanity, and other life forms. So we live our lives in contradiction. But we are finding new ways of describing ourselves, more by what we think and do than by what positions we occupy in categories of class, race, ethnicity, gender, or revolutionary grouping.[8] For instance, as the Zapatistas and other revolutionaries in the global South emphasize, we cherish our dignity, feel dignified rage, and no longer will tolerate attacks against our dignity from the hierarchies of capitalism. We under-

---

7 Helpful accounts of these revolutions are: Andrej Grubacic and Denis O'Hearn, *Living at the Edges of Capitalism: Adventures in Exile and Mutual Aid* (Oakland, CA: University of California Press, 2016), section 4; Dylan Eldredge Fitzwater, *Autonomy Is in Our Hearts: Zapatista Autonomous Government through the Lens of the Tsotsil Language* (Oakland, CA: PM Press, 2019); and Thomas Schmidinger, *The Battle for the Mountain of the Kurds: Self-Determination and Ethnic Cleansing in the Afrin Region of Rojava* (Oakland, CA: PM Press, 2019).
8 John Holloway, *In, Against, and Beyond Capitalism: The San Francisco Lectures* (Oakland, CA: PM Press, 2016).

stand that, although poor, we are the source of "their" wealth, and that understanding leads us to rebel. We do not fit into capitalist society. Although we work for capitalism, we struggle against capitalist work and the "bullshit jobs" that it makes us do to survive.[9] We strive to work creatively outside the exploitation and deskilling of the capitalist workplace.

No longer will we accept being dominated by the rich and powerful, knowing that they can only dominate us if we give our consent. As a respected and controversial thinker and revolutionary puts it, "We are the crisis of capitalism, and we are proud of it."[10] Or, as a group of young Rustbelt revolutionaries declared in a mission statement for social media, "We are the termites that advance the decaying of bourgeois institutions, and we are the builders that will build new ones from grassroots people power."[11]

Given the devastation that capitalism has caused, we no longer can defer revolutionary transformation. The crises and weaknesses of capitalism have become ever more profound. Capitalism's inherent contradictions are the main reasons for this frailty, especially the need for constant growth despite the limited resources that the earth can provide. As Ernest Mandel wrote, capitalism "is condemned to die sooner or later. But it will...always be necessary to give it a conscious little push...and it is our job ... to do the pushing."[12]

---

9   David Graeber, *Bullshit Jobs: A Theory* (New York: Simon & Schuster, 2018).
10 Holloway, *In, Against, and Beyond Capitalism*, part 3; John Holloway, *We Are the Crisis of Capital* (Oakland, CA: PM Press, 2019).
11 Horizontal Stateline Autonomous Region, "About," https://www.facebook.com/HorizontalStateline/.
12 Ernest Mandel, *An Introduction to Marxist Economic History* (Chippendale,

So what is that revolutionary "conscious little push"?

That little push requires that we clarify what characteristics of capitalism are oppressive and have to go. Those noxious attributes include: the exploitation and expropriation of humans (especially women and socially constructed racial minorities), animals, and nature; capitalists' extraction of surplus value from workers' labor due to ownership of the means of production, which is the inherent, structural basis of exploitation under capitalism, without which capitalism can't exist, even with friendly, well-meaning capitalists in charge; the requirement of economic growth, leading to recurrent crises of overproduction, economic surplus, under-employment, starvation in the midst of plenty, and environmental devastation (a statement widely attributed to the economist Kenneth Boulding argued, "Anyone who believes in indefinite growth on a physically finite planet is either mad or an economist"); racism and sexism that "they" use to confuse, divide, oppress, and discourage us from uniting; imperialism, which dominates peoples around the world mostly in the global South, for the benefit of a tiny minority mostly in the global North; and militarism, which always stands behind economic domination and now has become, through endless war and the global arms trade, one of few key ways to accumulate massive amounts of capital. We need to figure out and then implement the elements of the conscious little push: concrete actions to slow down and bring to a stop the processes that capitalism requires to survive.

Australia: Resistance Books, 2002), part 2, https://www.marxists.org/archive/mandel/1967/intromet/index.htm.

These actions target those contradictions where capitalism is the most vulnerable: what John Holloway calls the "cracks" of capitalism.[13]

Clarifying what characteristics of social and economic organization are not oppressive and don't have to go also helps in the conscious little push. These items have caused confusion, misconceptions, and lies about what post-capitalist society will look like. In post-capitalism private property that does not involve expropriating nature or extracting surplus value from others' labor can stay. Okay private property includes items like homes, gardens, eco-friendly cars, and personal possessions, although conspicuous consumption likely will receive some frowns. Small non-exploitative businesses, co-ops, credit unions, etc., also will be okay forms of post-capitalist private property. In contrast to some prior socialist countries that actually came to practice a form of state capitalism, such as the Soviet Union, creative and non-creative differences among individuals and groups, including variation of abilities and potentials, can stay and even be nurtured. Constructive criticism and self-criticism become highly valued contributions.

Given that there is a "world to build," what is that world?[14] Worthy visions of post-capitalist society include a better understanding of what that society is and is not. Based on disappointments following most prior revolutionary transformations, we know what

---

13 John Holloway, *Crack Capitalism* (London: Pluto Press, 2010).
14 Marta Harnecker, *A World To Build* (New York: Monthly Review Press, 2015), especially chapters 7-9; Harnecker and Bartolomé, *Planning from Below*.

post-capitalist society will not include: a vanguard elite, Stalinist types of repression, a police state, uniformity without tolerance for individual differences or disagreements, and re-emergence of new classes or similar hierarchies. Resolution of inevitable conflicts, when they occur, will not involve violence or threats of violence.

What post-capitalist society looks like has become clearer than those images expressed by our forefathers and foremothers (Marx, Engels, Rosa Luxemburg, Lenin, and some others). Post-capitalism builds on ecosocialist-feminist and indigenous principles, including communal governance and mutual aid. While seeking to resolve contradictions based on gender, racism, and other socially constructed differences, post-capitalism also prevents the re-emergence of social class hierarchies based on access to arms, bureaucratic control over the means of production even without private ownership, differential knowledge and skill, or other characteristics that lead to domination. Communities take responsibility for safety and eliminate access to guns and other weapons on a day-to-day basis (as some countries currently do already). Economic activities are non-capitalist, meaning that they do not extract surplus value from workers who sell their labor to survive. Instead, "living well"—a model of life after capitalism that is gaining ground worldwide, even in the new constitutions of some nations—happens by creating goods and services within a solidarity economy, based on cooperation and mutual aid.[15] The econ-

---

15 Consejo Nacional de Planificación, *Buen Vivir: Plan Nacional,* 2013-2017 (Quito, Ecuador: Government of Ecuador, 2013), https://www.unicef.org/ecuador/Plan_Nacional_Buen_Vivir_2013-2017.pdf; Fernando Huanacuni

omy aims not to grow but rather to sustain the earth and those who live here. Assuring everyone's comfortable survival, especially by solving the perpetual challenges of finding a place to live and feeding oneself and others who depend on us, becomes the economy's main goal. Energy comes from sources other than carbon, uranium, and plutonium. Work involves more creative fun and fosters personal development. Technology reduces time needed for work and expands leisure time. Amazingly, fear and anxiety in daily life give way to...happiness, not always but usually. Wow!

Isn't that worth spending some time and energy to answer the question about how to get from A to B, and then to act on the answers? Without claims that they are the only answers, here are a few possibilities at least to start, plus an invitation to talk and to walk along the path or paths to survival and living well. The humdrum revolutionary opportunities that follow flow not from abstract theory but from praxis, the combining of theory and practice. Thousands and probably millions of people worldwide have begun to enact these and similar forms of praxis, and as this revolution grows, it can't be stopped. Yes, the handful with fingers on nuclear triggers could stop it, but they won't, because they have too much real estate to lose if they do.

Mamani, "BOLIVIA-Buen Vivir/Vivir Bien. Los 13 principios," https://caminantedelsur.com/2018/02/05/bolivia-buen-vivir-vivir-bien-los-13-principiospor-fernando-huanacuni-mamani/; Chris Hartmann, "Buen Vivir (Living Well): Implications for Public Health in Latin America and Globally," University of Florida, April 11, 2018, http://epi.ufl.edu/onehealth/seminars/specialseminars/, and "'Live Beautiful, Live Well' (*Vivir Bonito, Vivir Bien*) in Nicaragua: Environmental Health Citizenship in a Post-Neoliberal Context," *Global Public Health* 14, no. 6-7 (August 2018), https://doi.org/10.1080/17441692.2018.1506812.

Radical transformations call for simple, safe, and rinky-dink actions and inactions. These include withholding consent to processes that capitalism needs to maintain itself and grow, as well as several creatively constructive and destructive efforts in which millions of people, but still a minority of the population, participate (Figures 2 and 2a. Figure 2a expands the bottom boxes about the rinky-dink revolution.)

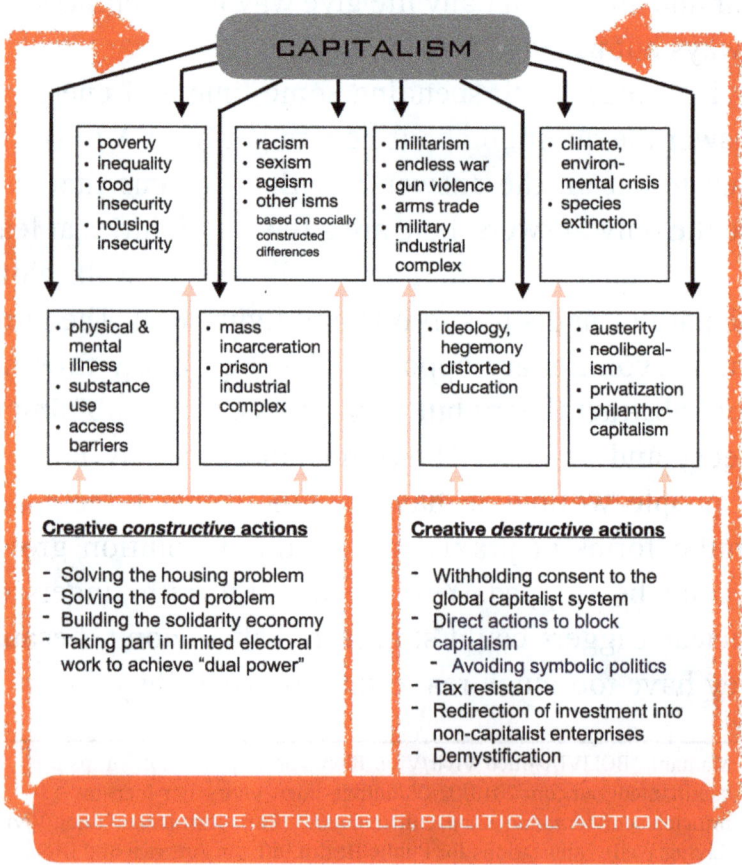

Figure 2. Rinky-Dink Revolution: Struggling to Improve Our Key Problems By Confronting and Moving Beyond Capitalism

```
                    ┌─────────────────┐
                    │   CAPITALISM    │
                    └─────────────────┘
                             ▲
                             │
┌──────────────────────────┐ │ ┌──────────────────────────┐
│ **Creative *constructive* actions** │ │ **Creative *destructive* actions** │
│                          │ │ │                          │
│ - Solving the housing problem │ │ - Withholding consent to the │
│ - Solving the food problem    │ │   global capitalist system │
│ - Building the solidarity     │ │ - Direct actions to block │
│   economy                │ │ │   capitalism             │
│ - Taking part in limited │ │ │   - Avoiding symbolic politics │
│   electoral work to achieve │ │ - Tax resistance         │
│   "dual power"           │ │ │ - Redirection of investment │
│                          │ │ │   into non-capitalist    │
│                          │ │ │   enterprises            │
│                          │ │ │ - Demystification        │
└──────────────────────────┘ │ └──────────────────────────┘
                             │
┌────────────────────────────────────────────────────────┐
│  RESISTANCE, STRUGGLE, POLITICAL ACTION                │
└────────────────────────────────────────────────────────┘
```

Figure 2a. Rinky-Dink Revolution: Struggling to Improve Our Key Problems By Confronting and Moving Beyond Capitalism

Creative **constructions**

One main way to begin the transition to post-capitalism is to start living as though the transition is already happening, and it actually is happening. This transition isn't happening through elections of bourgeois democracy, which have never led to social transformation. The national political parties in the United States and other capitalist nations will not lead this transition. Instead, the transition is happening throughout the world in the construction of communal organizations that govern themselves and that act to assure the survival and well-being of their participants. Moving beyond the capitalist state, including the welfare state as part of the capitalist state, entails moving beyond the state itself. Such a transition beyond the state has been the eventual goal of revolutions spanning Marxism, anarchism, and their many variations. Building communal organizations and governance has emerged as an important path beyond capitalism and the capitalist state.

Nearly everywhere you go in the world today, you can see and participate in such post-capitalist communal organizations. Their clearest expressions have happened in places like Venezuela (influenced partly by the theory of transition beyond capital that Mészáros developed and that Hugo Chávez and his comrades have tried to implement against great odds), Chiapas and Bolivia (shaped by indigenous concepts of community and mutual aid), and Rojava in northern Syria (affected by Kurdish principles of community, anarchist theories of communalism, and revolutionary feminism). Because communal governance provides a viable alternative to the global capitalist political-economic system, these

Cooperation Jackson

Building a solidarity economy in Jackson, Mississippi, anchored by a network of cooperatives and worker-owned, democratically self-managed enterprises.

Jackson Rising: building the solidarity economy in Mississippi. From roots in African-American organizing within the deep South and principles of nationalism and grassroots power developed by activists like Malcolm X, Jackson Rising focuses on housing, food independence and environmental sustainability.

cooperationjackson.org

struggles have endured attack after attack, but they continue. Communal organizations also have thrived or are struggling to grow in areas where few if any other options exist, because they are the most affected by neoliberal policies such as austerity and precarious employment, including Greece, Spain, multiple communities in Latin America, and more than two hundred places in the United States.¹ These efforts emphasize the goal of "living well," expressed in various ways (for instance, sumak kawsay in Quechua, or buen vivir in Spanish, as developed in Latin American countries like Bolivia that have adopted this goal as a key component of national health policies linked to new national constitutions). Living well usually implies community-based solidarity and sustainability through "mutual aid," moving away from the social conditions of capitalist society that worsen poverty, inequality, environmental pollution, and unacceptable health outcomes.²

Most of these efforts aim to free people from spending most of our lives as workers in precarious, proletarianized, bullshit jobs, where we are unable to survive with healthy lives, let alone to feel a sense of accomplishment in work or solidarity in community. One way of describing this struggle is to reduce the need to work as "wage slaves", without energy and time to create a new and different world. Moving into a post-capitalist world means finding solutions to some age-old problems.

First, groups trying to achieve a solidarity economy develop ways to solve the housing problem. For most

---

1 Among the many examples of organizations active in this transition, two provide ongoing information about struggles worldwide to build the post-capitalist economy: the New Economy Coalition (https:// neweconomy.net/) and the Schumacher Center for a New Economics (https:// centerforneweconomics.org). These organizations usually refer to a "new economy" rather than a "post-capitalist economy", partly to broaden participation and to avoid conflict based on misunderstood words. In these networks a transition beyond capitalism becomes a unifying goal.
2 See note 15 in the previous chapter 'Rinky-Dink Revolution and Revolutionaries'. Regarding mutual aid, the biologist Peter Kropotkin made observations in the anarchist tradition that have influenced recent directions of "living well"; see *Mutual Aid* (Boston: Extending Horizon Books, 1914), chapters 7 and 8.

Horizontal Stateline Autonomous Region

Building the solidarity economy in the rust belt of the Midwest, "Horizontal" builds on anarcho-socialist principles that achieve democratic and communal self-governance without a hierarchical state apparatus, as modeled in the Zapatista revolution in southern Mexico and the Rojava revolution in northern Syria.

facebook.com/horizontalstateline

Community gardens, cooperative local food production: scenes from the Horizontal Stateline Autonomous Region

people, paying for housing becomes the biggest expense requiring us to labor for wages in the capitalist economy and also becomes a main source of day-to-day insecurity. So, the solidarity economy first of all finds ways to create cheap, small-scale, cooperative, pleasant, and comfortable housing units that require very little money, with collaborative solutions to avoid the exploitative conditions that capitalism imposes on people who need housing, such as rent, debt, taxes, and insurance. Housing co-ops find inexpensive properties in cities or rural areas where housing can be rehabilitated or constructed with sweat labor and the increasingly sophisticated technologies (tiny homes, 3-D printing, and so forth) that reduce costs and improve the environmental sustainability of housing materials.[3] Initial financing can come from multiple creative sources and proves less challenging than expected (more below under "creative destructions" about the part coming from individual investments). The aim is about $150 per person per month of housing costs, which can be in dollars, local currency of a city or town, or non-monetary time equivalents of donated work (called by such names as "Mutual Exchange of Work" units, or "MEOWs").[4]

Secondly, the path to a solidarity economy includes solving the food problem. The goal is sustainable, local food production and consumption with a low carbon footprint (meaning minimal petroleum products used

---

3 For further information about Cooperation Jackson's path-breaking efforts in Mississippi, see: Akuno and Nangwaya, *Jackson Rising*.
4 The Schumacher Center has compiled worldwide resources on alternative currency and non-monetary exchange approaches: https://centerforneweconomics. org/apply/local-currencies-program/localcurrenciesdirectory/mutualcredit/.

for fertilizers, pesticides, and transportation of food and its raw materials) and with a more favorable impact on the health of human beings, other living species, and the earth. Community gardens and food coops figure as key components of achieving food security, a critical goal for obvious reasons. Gardening principles include cultivating plants that produce healthy nutrients such as non-animal sources of proteins, with limited sugar and fat. These principles recognize the worldwide epidemics of obesity and diabetes, which reflect a combination of food insecurity, "food deserts" where healthy foods are unavailable or too expensive for purchase in many inner-city and rural areas, and over-promotion of sugar- and fat-rich foods by capitalist agricultural and food industries that manufacture and market processed foods. Animals providing meat, fish, eggs, and milk products for human beings who opt for continuing non-vegetarian or non-vegan diets are locally raised, slaughtered, and packaged for local consumption. A key objective is independence from capitalist agriculture. Food independence means giving up consumption of food that requires access to seasonal production in distant places with carbon-based transportation over long distances, whose high costs and pollution contribute to the climate crisis, depletion of fresh water, and continuing exploitation of agricultural workers. For families of average size, the aim again is $150 per month of food costs, which can be in currency or time equivalents.[5]

---

[5] Again, the efforts of Cooperation Jackson offer helpful perspectives on sustainable food production and distribution: Akuno and Nangwaya, *Jackson Rising*.

Other key elements of living well in the solidarity economy involve stopping economic activities that are ecologically unsustainable.[6] Capitalism's inherent need for growth requires endless expropriation of natural resources and pollution of the planet. Thus, constructing the solidarity economy outside capitalism fosters de-growth, which means stopping the vicious cycle of overproduction and overconsumption that inherently damage the earth and its beings. Economic growth requires consent at the level of desire. Ideology, as already discussed, fosters desire for unneeded consumer goods and services, and manipulated desire fuels the demand leading to unnecessary overproduction. Breaking this vicious cycle of growth involves stopping our consent to it, requiring shifts in the desires that capitalist markets have generated.

Transportation provides a clear example of withholding consent to unsustainable economic activities. As one of many examples, each roundtrip transcontinental airplane flight generates a carbon footprint that leads to the melting of about three cubic meters of arctic ice.[7] So going beyond capitalism, among other activities that produce carbon dioxide, requires not seeing so much of the world so much of the time. Similar undramatic choices involve the vehicles we choose to use every day.

---

6 For helpful discussions of the expropriation/ robbery of nature as an inherent characteristic of the capitalist economic system, see: John Bellamy Foster and Brett Clark, "The Expropriation of Nature," *Monthly Review* 69, no. 10 (March 2018): 1-27; and "The Robbery of Nature," *Monthly Review* 70, no. 3 (July-August 2018): 1-20.

7 Dirk Notz and Julienne Stroeve, "Observed Arctic Sea-Ice Loss Directly Follows Anthropogenic CO_2 Emission," *Science* 54 (2016): 747-50.

Simple changes in economic consumption, of course, will not save the planet without other revolutionary actions that withhold consent to capitalism's ways of doing business, some of which appear below in the section on creative destructions.

Will we need money in post-capitalism? Day-to-day life in the solidarity economy means engaging in cooperative economic activities to meet one's own needs and wants, as well as meeting the needs and wants of others in one's community. Interestingly, one doesn't need money for many of these post-capitalist economic activities. Communities all over the world are discovering and implementing local economies that do not require much if any national currency such as dollars. Instead, people are returning to simpler versions of economic transactions, where goods and services are produced and exchanged directly at the local level. The transactions in these post-capitalist markets involve products that are not commodities in Marx's sense, because the products' value does not include a component of surplus value produced by workers but received by capitalists. Instead, transactions based on the products' use value in daily life become the norm.[8] As many affected by austerity already have learned, such transactions lead to an understanding that we really do not need global capitalism. We can live and thrive without the one percent easier than they can without us.

Several examples of non-capitalist economic activities are becoming more common. Through barter, people

---

[8] Always helpful on these distinctions is: Karl Marx, *Capital*, volume 1, parts 3-5, https://www.marxists.org/archive/marx/works/download/pdf/Capital-Volume-I.pdf.

can directly exchange a good or service, satisfying what each person needs or wants; barter can include simple products and services, or more complex ones like those provided by health and mental health professionals, educators, people with legal training, information technologists, and so forth. Alternatively, with time banking, a person can do one hour of work anywhere in a specified community of participants; after one person provides one hour of work, he or she can request one hour of work from the time bank, which coordinates requests for services and keeps track of time worked. Again, specialized services like those provided by health and mental health co-ops can happen at the community level within a time bank framework; practitioners provide services they are trained to offer and, in return, receive goods and services that they need. Communities also can create their own local currencies, which people use to exchange goods and services. Within many communities, people are deciding to share their infrastructure, including tools, kitchens, libraries, workspaces, equipment, communication facilities such as phones and internet, and buildings for housing, stores, clinics, hospitals, and other facilities that respond to common needs and wants. Such spaces become components of a "commons," which is available for everyone to share but does not generate profits that some people can enjoy at the expense of others.

What is the role of "electoral democracy" in the solidarity economy? Not much. Communities worldwide that are trying to construct economies not dependent on or dominated by the global capitalist system have developed a profound skepticism about the capitalist state, and this skepticism applies also to the feasibility of successful and enduring systems managed by the welfare state component of the capitalist state. As one among many examples, rather than investing time, money, and energy in national electoral politics and politicians to advance goals like a national health program (NHP), activists have realized that non-capitalist NHPs cannot survive without social movements that transform the fundamental characteristics of capitalism itself.

Because this understanding applies especially to elections, the focus moves from the national and state levels to the local level, usually the county or municipality. Activists take part in limited electoral work to achieve "dual power" at the local level, but without illusions about elections and with clarity about the effects of elections through history. As implemented most clearly by Cooperation Jackson, dual power involves two elements. First, to summarize briefly, activists build a network of strong community-based organizations that focus on different components of the solidarity economy (such as housing, food, ecologically sustainable energy production and waste management, transportation, education, and health and mental health services), and that make decisions by direct participatory discussion and consensus within a "communal" structure. Adapting their model from revolutionary struggles in other countries and theories of transition beyond the capitalist state, local communes eventually assume the main responsibility for governance in post-capitalist society and choose the regional leaders who implement policies shaped mostly from below.⁹

Secondly, during a transitional period, activists prioritize winning local elections, especially for mayor and municipal or county councils, as has occurred in Jackson. Local elections accomplish some narrow purposes. One key purpose involves the prevention of repression and brutality by police and other wings of "law enforcement" at various levels of government, and by those outside government who take justice into their own hands through gun violence, paramilitary actions, and other forms of victimization. Another key purpose involves access to funds and labor based in the public sector to help provide housing, food, and needed services including water, electricity, heat, sanitation, fire protection, public education, and health and mental health services that, in the short term, community residents cannot fully provide by themselves.[10]

---

9 For more on transition from the capitalist state to postcapitalist participatory governance, see note 4 in chapter 'Moving beyond capitalism now'. A similar model of communal governance but with more anarchist roots has emerged in the autonomous region of Rojava in northern Syria, as part of the so-called Rojava Revolution. See, for instance, note 7 in chapter "Rinky-dink revolution and revolutionaries", and Michael Knapp, Anja Flach, and Ercan Ayboga, *Revolution in Rojava: Democratic Autonomy and Women's Liberation in Syrian Kurdistan* (London: Pluto Press, 2016), chapters 5-7, 11-13.
10 Akuno and Nangwaya, *Jackson Rising*.

Creative
destructions

Even if violent revolutions to overcome capitalism happen in the United States or other capitalist countries, it is very unlikely that they will succeed, and this is not news. Despite romantic visions about the military capabilities of revolutionaries like Che Guevara, the militarization of capitalist societies has become so profound that devastating post-revolutionary repression of revolutionary violence appears much more probable than a transition to post-capitalism. The historical track record of violent revolutions against capitalism and imperialism, in terms of long-term viability, is underwhelming. With the possible exception of Cuba, the challenges of building socialism after revolutionary war within a capitalist world system so far have proven insurmountable. Among the disappointing examples, the Vietnamese people won the military conflict but then arguably lost the war to the International Monetary Fund and World Bank. Plus, fear of violence and its consequences demotivates many revolutionaries for good reason, so arguments favoring violent revolt usually seem half-hearted. And then revolutionaries who conscientiously object to war (like me, as a card-carrying conscientious objector, "CO") can't extinguish our moral anguish about killing other sentient beings for whatever reason.

Are there examples of non-violent revolutions that stand a prayer of success? That is, can a small minority of a country's population, say the 3.5 to 5 percent mentioned earlier, bring about revolutionary change? Yes! In fact, all the revolutions currently in progress worldwide are non-violent in essence. In the communal organizations of Chiapas, Rojava, Venezuela, Bolivia, Greece, the Rustbelt of the U.S. Midwest, and many other places, some revolutionaries dedicated to non-violent revolution do bear arms, but to my knowledge they use these arms only for defensive purposes, in case of attack by counterrevolutionaries, forces of imperialism, or drug cartels; most revolutionaries in these places do not bear arms at all. Despite internal and external attempts to reverse their achievements, these revolutions persist and potentially even grow — if they are not crushed by reaction.

Creative destructions through revolutionary non-violence do not take place by obtaining police permits for demonstrations, even huge ones, but rather by actually slowing down or stopping the smooth functioning of capitalism. Efforts to reduce use of fossil fuels, plastics, foods and other products that require petroleum to reach us over long distance, and so forth, motivate helpful changes in consumption. But reducing consumption will exert little impact on capitalism unless processes of capitalist production are blocked. Among many guides for revolution, indigenous communities provide illuminating examples of non-violent tactics that confront capitalism directly, and such examples are inspiring non-indigenous communities to take similar actions.[1]

An inspirational example is the heroic struggle at Standing Rock to stop the Dakota Access Pipeline. Thousands of participants from indigenous and non-indigenous communities around the world came to take part

---

1 Nick Estes, *Our History Is the Future: Standing Rock Versus the Dakota Access Pipeline, and the Long Tradition of Indigenous Resistance* (New York: Penguin Random House, 2019); Waitzkin, "Revolution Now."

in these actions. Here the explicit purposes were not just to demonstrate against a monstrous, last-ditch effort to accumulate massive profits by robbing indigenous lands, polluting water supplies, and worsening the climate crisis by burning oil. Protecting indigenous lands and communities, preserving accessibility of safe water supplies, and addressing the social and environmental determinants of illness and early death were fundamental goals. However, the Standing Rock actions also aimed to stop the pipeline's construction and to block transport of oil to refineries and eventually to consumers. In other words, a key goal was to slow down and to halt an important component needed for the smooth functioning of the capitalist economic system. Brutal repression ended one phase of this struggle.

But such struggles to protect the earth and its beings by obstructing the infrastructure and day-to-day operations of capitalism persist and grow. Similar heroic, non-violent movements by indigenous communities to block oil extraction and transport have emerged in the United States, Canada, Latin America, Africa, and other regions. Inspired partly by these actions, non-indigenous communities affected by pipelines also are rising up, leading to time-consuming and expensive efforts by the petroleum industry and their financial backers in the FIRE industry to orchestrate deepening repression. Tactically, these experiences lead to the realization that direct actions can disrupt business as usual, even if disrupters disperse when they receive warnings that they are about to be arrested. Despite efforts by executives and their legislative cronies to expand laws and regulations that restrict non-violent resistance, legalities do require warnings by police and military forces before arrests or physical attacks begin. Latin American revolutionaries have shown that blocking a pipeline, highway, railroad, port, or airport for quite a long time does not necessarily imply the need to block it until arrest or injury.[2]

In direct actions that target transport of fossil fuels, toxic chemicals, conventional and nuclear weapons, military equipment, precious metals, timber, and other items that keep the capitalist system afloat, actions that move from place to place quickly interrupt the system's smooth flow more than demonstrations that risk arrest and injuries for the sake of non-disruptive symbolism. Even when resisters get arrested, while we do experience some inconvenience, jail time usually is brief, and trying to save the planet has become an acceptable defense even in some U.S. courts. Direct actions like these become creative destructions of capitalism that, as they grow, provide one piece of the "little push" to which the crisis-ridden economic system has become vulnerable.

Although such direct actions are not very risky, other creative destructions to push capitalism down bring even less risk, because they mostly involve direct inactions rather than actions. Such inactions focus on stopping our consent to financial processes that capitalism needs to survive. Revolutionaries can change what we do with our money, especially in the realms of investments, taxes, and local economic activities. Such changes disrupt, undermine, and create space for

---

[2] Waitzkin, "Revolution Now."

further revolutionary actions. As the main funders of capitalism, we consent as our money flows to corporations that exploit workers, destroy nature, raise the earth's temperature, and keep us in permanent war and perpetual inequality. We need to change our habits of giving up our money. If enough of us do that, those who control the capitalist economy and capitalist state no longer will be able to prop up the economic system for the benefit of the ultra-rich.

First, let's focus on day-to-day financial transactions and investments. What we do with our money helps corporations and the FIRE industry achieve the goals that we hate. For instance, those sad effects happen when we pay our credit card bills, mortgages, and car loans and when we save in our little bank or retirement accounts. That money flows into big banks and other finance corporations that then loan the money or invest in corporations that build the Dakota Access Pipeline, manufacture arms, operate privatized prisons and schools, produce and market pharmaceuticals, and sell private health insurance policies. They, rather than our friends, neighbors, and comrades, benefit from our financial choices. Even if we invest in so-called "socially conscious" funds, the purportedly "clean" capitalist companies that receive our money include the drug, insurance, and technology sectors, rather than "dirty" tobacco and oil companies. And if we try to persuade our cities, universities, and other institutional investors to divest from banks and corporations that support Israel, pipelines, oil companies, and other bastions of capitalism, we don't see that we as millions of individuals and families are actually more important as aggregated investors than any of the institutional investors that we try to influence.

What would happen if we change our financial habits? For instance, it never fails to amaze me that progressive organizations and comrades (and even myself in the past) often do savings and checking accounts, credit cards, car and home loans, and retirement accounts through Citibank, Chase, Bank of America, Wells Fargo, Fidelity, Goldman Sachs, and capitalism's other delightful bulwarks. Sometimes we do that for such motives as obtaining free flights that increase our carbon footprints and destroy more arctic ice. If we move some of that money into local, non-profit credit unions, at least they use most of it to help us and our neighbors buy affordable housing and invest in local food production. In this way, fewer funds circulate through the global capitalist financial system, leading to less concentrated wealth for the ultra-rich, less inequality, and more usable financial resources within our communities.

Now let's say we go one step further and take some money out of the capitalist economy altogether by directly investing in local housing and food production. Most of the 7 to 11 million revolutionaries we've been talking about wouldn't be able to do that, because they have hardly enough money to get by, let alone to invest. According to the Federal Reserve, 40 percent of U.S. adults could not pay an unexpected expense of $400, over one-fourth skipped needed medical care because they couldn't afford the cost, fewer than 40 percent believe that they will have enough savings to retire, and 25 percent report no retirement savings or pension whatsoever.³ We really can't expect our fellow revolutionaries to be better off than that.

But some folks like me have lived more years on the planet, have worked and gotten paid for some of them, and don't feel a need to spend much money. We have saved some nest eggs in credit unions or in retirement funds that money managers like TIAA invest somewhere unpleasant in the global capitalist financial system, for which they pay us a very small rate of return. Let's say that some of us take a portion of that money and use it to buy housing so our young comrades and maybe we ourselves can live cooperatively on $150 a month each, and also buy some land so we can produce most of the fresh, canned, dried, or frozen food we need to eat throughout the year at a cost of $150 a month each. If 2 million of us revolutionaries, much fewer than the 7 to 11 million we've been mentioning, set aside $20,000 to invest in such housing and food production, we could devote $40 billion for those purposes without hardship. That is about 3 percent of the entire 2020 federal budget for human resources and about 34 percent of the federal budget for physical resources. It also totals about twice the profits of private health insurance corporations in 2017.⁴

---

3 Board of Governors of the Federal Reserve System, "Report on the Economic Well-Being of U.S. Households in 2017 - May 2018," https://www.federalreserve.gov/publications/2018-economic-well-being-of-us-households-in-2017-executive-summary.htm.

4 Human resources include the Departments of Health and Human Services, Social Security Administration, Education, food and nutrition programs, Housing and Urban Development, Labor, and earned income, child, and

Disclosure: Here's a little story about trying to walk this talk. My partner Mira and I recently spent $75,000 of savings in a local credit union to buy 10 acres of lovely farmland, which this year is feeding members of the Horizontal Stateline Autonomous Region and other community residents who need food. We and others also have set aside more money to help buy Horizontal's first building for co-op housing. In our local urban housing market, we can get a fixer upper (including enough fixing so it's comfortably livable) to house eight people for about $60 thousand. We can do this partly because we look where others don't, in parts of town that aren't desirable to some, even to developers wanting to accumulate capital through gentrification, but actually are vibrant communities that welcome people trying to build a solidarity economy. Finding such opportunities is pretty easy in places like the Rustbelt and Jackson, Mississippi, but actually is possible in most areas if you look with a point of view that cherishes moving beyond capitalism.

In addition to the fun of moving our financial transactions, savings, and investments away from the capitalist

---

health insurance credits for those departments). Physical resources comprise the Departments of Agriculture, Interior, Transportation, Homeland Security [partial], Housing and Urban Development, Commerce, Energy [nonmilitary], NASA, Environmental Protection, National Science Foundation, Army Corps of Engineers, Federal Communications Commission, and health insurance credits for those departments. Data on the U.S. federal budget come from the War Resisters League (WRL), which does a detailed analysis and pie chart each fiscal year with a purpose of clarifying the money budgeted for war versus other purposes; 47 percent of the budget pays for past and present military expenditures. WRL explains the methodology and findings at this website: https://www.warresisters.org/resources/pie-chart-flyers-where-your-income-tax-money-really-goes. Data on the profits of the insurance industry come from analyses by Physicians for a National Health Program (PNHP, https://pnhp.org/ member-resources/slideshows/).

banks, retirement fund managers, and other components of the FIRE industry, a second arena of creative destruction in the rinky-dink revolution involves taxes. Changing attitudes and behaviors around taxation comes from understanding that death still may be inevitable but, just as for the ultra-rich, taxes are not. Since at least World War I, some people have resisted taxes that pay for war, a few eventually going to prison but the vast majority, like me, suffering no substantial harm.[5]

Disclosure: Partly because I'm a CO, for more than ten years during and after the Vietnam War, I openly resisted half of my income taxes, roughly the proportion of taxes that pays for past and present wars. After that, I was starting to feel inconvenienced and a little bored by appeals and other bureaucratic procedures inside and outside the Internal Revenue Service (IRS), because of open tax resistance. At that point, I made a decision to avoid war taxes through loopholes rather than resistance of conscience. But starting in tax year 2017, the death and devastation caused by the endless wars of the United States led Mira and me to resume open tax resistance. Assuming that a person honestly reports her or his income, conscientiously resisting 50 percent of income taxes that go for war entails very little risk, can become fun especially when done with many other similarly minded folk, and even can help build a solidarity economy outside capitalism. How?

Detailed guidance about how to do safe and enjoyable tax resistance is easy to find at the websites of the

---

[5] For a short history of U.S. war tax resistance: https://www.warresisters.org/history-war-tax-resistance.

National War Tax Resistance Coordinating Committee (NWTRCC), the War Resisters League (WRL), and several other groups devoted to organizing for peace and against militarism.[6] Trained, experienced counselors make themselves available to advise and otherwise help people who decide to resist war taxes. As the NWTRCC demonstrates in their comprehensive explanations, people can choose among many ways to resist taxes, depending on values, commitment, and comfort zones. Well researched data also show that the risks associated with tax resistance are very small.[7]

But how likely is real suffering for tax resisters if we are honest about our incomes and follow the IRS's bureaucratic procedures rather than ignoring them? Extremely unlikely. NWTRCC and the IRS itself give comprehensive and detailed information verifying that low probability. Amazingly, NWTRCC documents that since World War II only two people ever have gone to jail for not paying war taxes. A small number of other people did do brief jail time but always for not filing tax returns or not divulging where they kept their assets. Among the very few examples of property seized because of war tax resistance—such as a house, car, or even a bicycle—the last known case happened about twenty years ago in 1999.[8]

One way to resist taxes is the path that I have chosen over the years and that Mira and I expect to implement for the foreseeable future. While employed,

---

6 https://nwtrcc.org; https://www.warresisters.org/wartax-resistance.
7 For further information about "consequences": https://nwtrcc.org/resist/consequences/war-taxresisters-taken-court/.
8 https://nwtrcc.org/resist/consequences/war-taxresisters-taken-court/.

I have legally reduced withholding to prevent the IRS from taking all my taxes before I had a chance to resist them. I have done this by figuring out (sometimes with help from a supportive tax accountant) about a reasonable number of withholding allowances to claim honestly for estimated itemized deductions. On Form 1040, Mira and I claim deductions related to business and other expenses, which is a standard procedure even for rich capitalists who resist taxes through loopholes. We report income accurately and calculate tax owed after subtracting the deducted amounts to which we are entitled. Then we pay half that amount, which we can send in all at once or on a payment plan with interest about the same or less than we can earn by leaving the money in a credit union. Several months after we file the tax return, the IRS usually but not always sends a letter asking for the remaining half of the tax. More months pass as we explain why doing that is morally unacceptable, and the IRS sends letters back that despite our views we still must pay taxes for war (as opposed to not fighting in war, for which conscientious objection is an acceptable excuse—an enduring contradiction in federal policies about the rights of COs).

Eventually the IRS gives a final determination that we do indeed owe the tax. With that determination, the IRS provides information about our appeal rights, within the IRS and then within the civil court system. Then, we appeal within the IRS and do it once more at a second level of appeal. After that, we sometimes appeal through two levels of tax court.[9] The time and

---

9 In principle, the IRS can fine a tax resister for "frivolous" deductions

energy needed to do the appeals seem manageable, because each letter gives variations of the same text. After delays of two to three years after the initial tax return, the IRS finally succeeds in taking part or all of the originally owed tax by garnishing our wages or levying a credit union account, usually at a cost to the capitalist state in terms of paid employees' time much higher than the amount of tax ultimately collected.

An important reason why repression by the U.S. government for conscientious tax resistance happens so rarely is that the IRS has suffered from extensive cutbacks of budget and personnel. These cuts have led to rampant understaffing and overwork for the staff members who remain. The IRS workforce declined from about 90,000 in 2012 to 73,000 at the end of fiscal year 2017—a decrease of 14.9 percent. Over the same time period, IRS annual operating expenditures fell from $13.5 billion to $11.5 billion. Only 31,000 IRS employees currently are available to examine all income tax returns from individuals, businesses, and other categories of taxpayers, which total more than 187 million. In calendar year 2016, these employees audited less than 1.1 million tax returns, about 0.5 percent of all returns filed, equaling about 35 audits per employee per year. Unless they ignore everyone else with possibly incorrect tax returns, these employees could not possibly audit more than a tiny percentage of war tax resisters, let

---

or appeals, but there are organized ways to prevent and respond to this tactic as needed (https://www.irs.gov/newsroom/frivolous-tax-arguments-completes-the-irs-dirty-dozen-list-of-tax-scamsfor-the-2015-filing-season). Many war tax resisters do not use the appeal process. Currently, the IRS rarely garnishes wages and rarely finds credit union accounts if kept in non-interest bearing accounts.

alone succeed in collecting resisted taxes through two to three years of correspondence and appeals within and outside the IRS.[10]

But the greatest joy of war tax resistance isn't about not paying taxes; it's about redirecting the resisted taxes for creatively constructive purposes. So tax resisters set up alternative funds, often using escrow accounts in credit unions. Into these accounts we deposit the money that we otherwise would pay as taxes for war. Usually the accounts retain a small amount of the resisted taxes to help resistors financially in the unlikely event that the IRS eventually succeeds in collecting a substantial amount of money from individuals' savings or earnings from work. The rest of the resisted taxes go to help community-based groups seeking to build a solidarity economy, or wanting to provide needed local services, or helping GIs get the health and mental health services that they need outside the military, or other good causes. Resisters redirect many thousands of resisted war tax dollars in these ways.[11] NWTRCC estimates that around 10,000 people resist war taxes in the United States each year, and as a result those people redirect a substantial but unknown about of money in creatively constructive ways.

What if the number of resisters increased to ten million, the number that we have been considering as a meaningful revolutionary force, but still a very small percentage of the population. Here is a ballpark esti-

---

10 *Internal Revenue Service Data Book, 2017*, https://www.irs.gov/pub/irs-soi/17databk.pdf, especially pp. 14-21, 31-43, 73-77.

11 For instance, in 2018 the Northern California People's Life Fund redirected $65 thousand: https://nwtrcc.org/PDFs/mtap0618.pdf.

mate. For FY 2017, the IRS collected about $569 billion in taxes from 151 million taxpayers. That is a rough average of $3,800 collected from each taxpayer. Let's say our stalwart ten million revolutionaries resisted and then redirected half of that average collected, or $1,900. That means we would generate in a year about $19 billion—which is 1.3 percent of the money for all human resources in the 2020 federal budget, or 2.8 percent of funds spent for public education in primary and secondary schools during 2014-15, or slightly less than the total profits of private health insurance corporations during 2017, and $5.5 billion more than the IRS's annual operating budget. Along with the $40 billion generated by 2 million people who redirect savings and investments in the ways already mentioned, divesting from war by resisting war taxes would generate a pretty big chunk of change to help "capitalize" the post-capitalist solidarity economy.

Where Your Income Tax Money Really Goes: U.S. Federal Budget, 2020 Fiscal Year

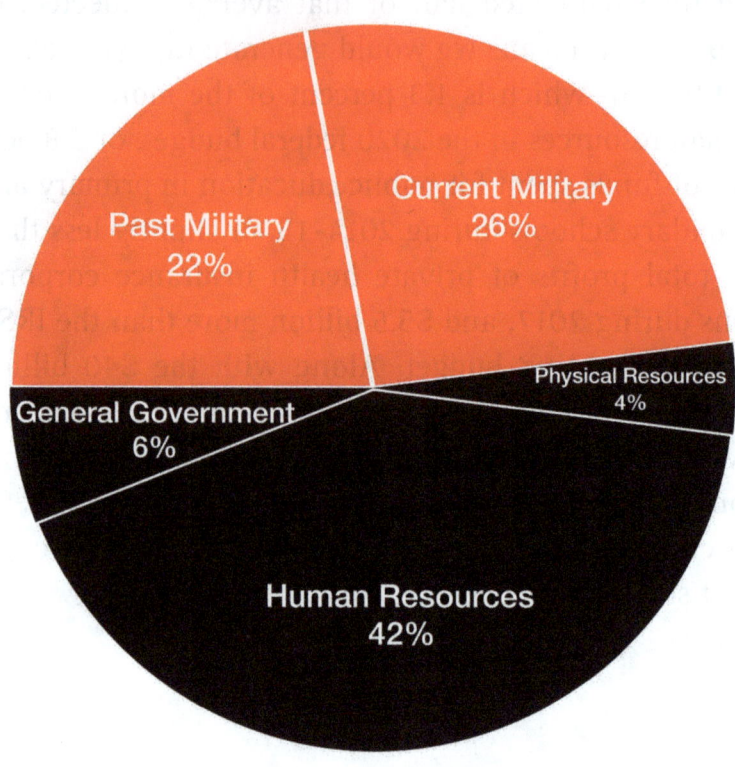

Source: War Resisters League. For methodology:
https://www.warresisters.org/sites/default/files/images/
fy2020pie_chart-low_res_bw.pdf

The death of capitalism
and the birth of something else

Rinky-dink revolution is simple, safe, and available to anyone who has the gumption to change her or his way of life a little bit. We can realize the joy of stopping our consent to and unwitting support for a system that we know destroys our well-being and happiness. The surprise will come when we see that revolution doesn't need to involve injury, death, or even much discomfort. It mainly requires that we stop doing a lot of things that we hate doing anyway.

Far from a revolutionary, T.S. Eliot began his poem "The Hollow Men" with epigraphs referring to Kurtz, the imperialist anti-hero of Joseph Conrad's *Heart of Darkness*, and to Guy Fawkes, the revolutionary leader of 1605 who conspired to bomb Parliament and centuries later became once again immortalized in the mask of the Occupy Movement.[1] Eliot published "The Hollow Men" in 1925, despairing about the condition of humanity in the aftermath of World War I and the financial bubble of the roaring 1920s. Eliot's friend and mentor, Ezra Pound, became one of Eliot's strongest influences during those years, partly through Pound's scathing criticism of finance capitalism.[2] While Eliot did not follow Pound into fascism, his depiction of the empty and purposeless "hollow men" became a profound image of capitalist society's leaders. Although Eliot's prediction about the end of the world has been

---

1 T. S. Eliot, "The Hollow Men," https://www.shmoop.com/ hollow-men/poem-text.html.
2 Pound's early poetic critique of usury appeared in "Canto XLV, With *Usura*" (1937), in *The Cantos of Ezra Pound* (New York: New Directions Publishing Company, 1993). Cantos during this time period included multiple disagreeable images of financial institutions under capitalism and favorable images of economic interactions based on mutual support and solidarity.

interpreted in several ways (including climate crisis, the great recession of 2008, and a stock market crash[3]), the whimper more persuasively refers to the death of capitalism and the birth of something else, after a necessary, inevitable, and victorious rinky-dink revolution:

This is the way the world ends
This is the way the world ends
This is the way the world ends
Not with a bang but a whimper.

---

3 Recession: https://www.theguardian.com/business/2009/jan/11/changing-square-mile); climate crisis (https://www.huffpost.com/entry/not-with-a-bang-buta-whi_b_40481); stock market: https://seekingalpha.com/article/3481286-t-s-eliot-stock-market-guru.

About the author

Howard Waitzkin is Distinguished Professor Emeritus of Sociology at the University of New Mexico and practices internal medicine part-time in New Mexico and Illinois. For many years he has been active in struggles focusing on health in the United States and Latin America. He is coordinator, with the Working Group for Health Beyond Capitalism, of *Health Care Under the Knife: Moving Beyond Capitalism for Our Health*, Monthly Review Press, 2018.

Acknowledgments

For their constructive suggestions, I thank Bradley Rydholm, Megan Devine, Summer Wagner, Mira Lee, Linda Raz, and David Black of Horizontal Stateline (https://www.facebook.com/HorizontalStateline/); Lincoln Rice of the National War Tax Resistance Coordinating Committee (https://nwtrcc.org); Martha Livingston and Johnathon Ross of the Socialist Caucus of the American Public Health Association (https://www.apha.org/apha-communities/caucuses/socialist-caucus); Firoze Manji of Daraja Press (https://darajapress.com); Brett Clark, John Bellamy Foster, and Camila Valle of *Monthly Review* (https://monthlyreview.org); and many friends and comrades in the Latin American Social Medicine Association (http://www.alames.org) who commented on a draft in the Association's congress during October 2018 in La Paz, Bolivia.

Vision statement: Moving beyond capitalism—now!

Howard Waitzkin and Firoze Manji

This publication represents a collaboration between Daraja Press and *Monthly Review* magazine.

We are living in revolutionary times. The present contains tremendous dangers: nuclear war, global warming and other environmental catastrophes, the condemnation of vast sections of humanity into sacrifice zones, and the growing threat of fascism—a world based on deepening expropriation of nature, inequality, repression, and suffering. These dangers have also generated global resistance and social movements aiming to end the rapacious features of capitalism, to create a world based on harmony with nature, cooperative relationships of mutual aid, and decision-making by ordinary people about the directions our societies will take.

The aim is to publish and distribute, in some instances as a collaboration between Daraja Press and *Monthly Review*, brief, easy-to-understand publications that present concrete proposals/manifestos for revolutionary actions that will help us move beyond the global capitalist political-economic system. Our vision is to produce clear, simply written, and creative manifestos in article or pamphlet formats, in the style of Thomas Paine's *Common Sense*, Karl Marx and Frederick Engels's *Communist Manifesto*, and Peter Kropotkin's *An Appeal to the Young*.

Both *Monthly Review* and Daraja Press will promote these publications through their networks and websites. The first publication, in what may become an ongoing series entitled *Moving Beyond Capitalism—Now!*, is Howard Waitzkin's *Rinky-Dink Revolution: Moving Beyond Capitalism by Withholding Consent, Creative Constructions, and Creative Destructions*. Some of the articles in this series, we hope, will address concretely how to move beyond capitalism in each problem area that is considered in the current pamphlet, such as environmental crisis, impoverishment and inequality, racism, sexism, militarism, health and mental health, incarceration, austerity, and related policies of neoliberalism. Other pamphlets may present approaches to the post-capitalist solidarity economy, media and communication, public services, and community organizing.

At the same time, Daraja Press plans to publish a series of pamphlets that are focused primarily on priority concerns for the global South as well as introductory texts on struggles of critical importance today, a series entitled *Thinking Freedom*. Not all such publications will be jointly published.

We invite you to consider submitting articles for the series. The length of each article, essay, pamphlet, or manifesto is flexible; in general we recommend no more than 12,000 words plus pertinent reference notes. Please use a style that is not academic and that ordinary folks can understand and find helpful for day-to-day decisions and actions.

If you would like to submit a piece for publication, please submit your proposal electronically, providing a title, synopsis, the primary readership to whom the pamphlet is aimed, and one paragraph on why this topic is important. Please also provide a half-page summary of your CV. Submit the materials at the same time to *Monthly Review* (mrmag@monthlyreview.org) and Daraja Press (info@darajapress.com). If you have questions, concerns, or suggestions, please write to us at the same addresses.

Howard Waitzkin is the author of *Rinky-Dink Revolution*.

Firoze Manji is publisher of Daraja Press.

www.ingramcontent.com/pod-product-compliance
Lightning Source LLC
Chambersburg PA
CBHW060033040426
42333CB00042B/2417